NELSON'S
WEST INDIAN READERS

First Primer

Compiled by J. O. Cutteridge

Nelson Thornes

LETTER SOUNDS

Note to Teacher.—The child should pronounce the name of the object and then emphasize the initial sound, *e.g. apple.* He then says " a !—a !—a ! " (as in the word), and so discovers the sound of the letter.

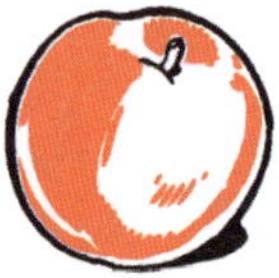	a	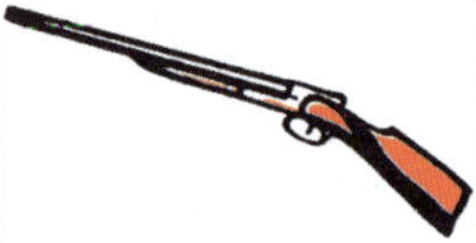	g
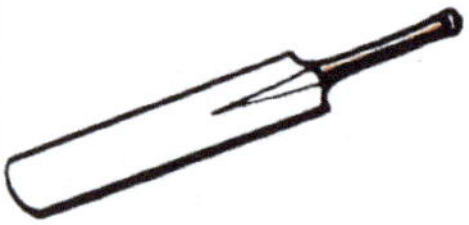	b	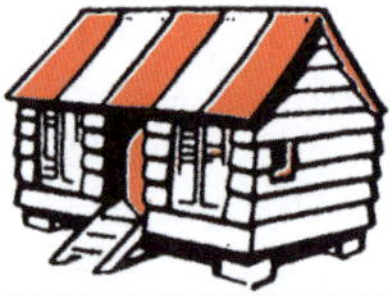	h
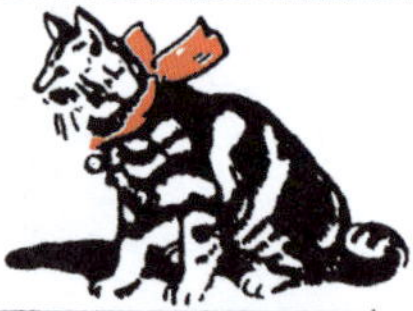	c	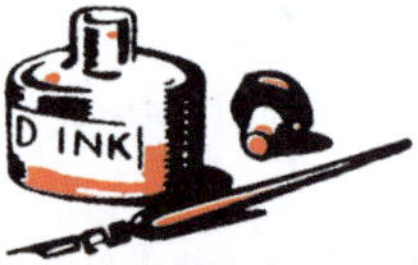	i
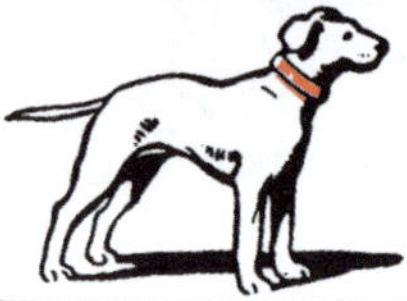	d	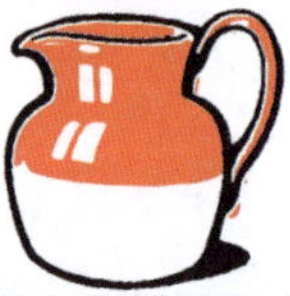	j
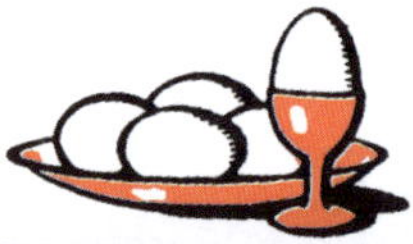	e	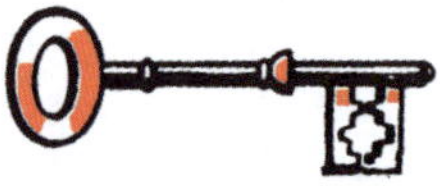	k
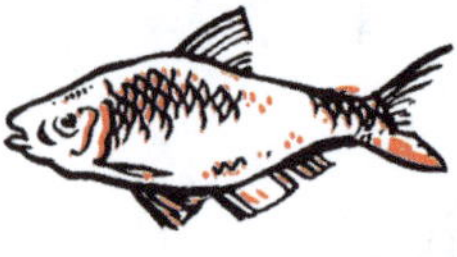	f	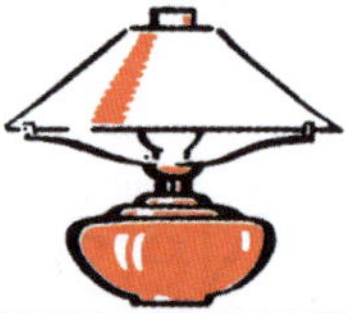	l

Note.—Names of letters can be learned gradually as the need for them arises.   Little attention need be given to this at present.

	m	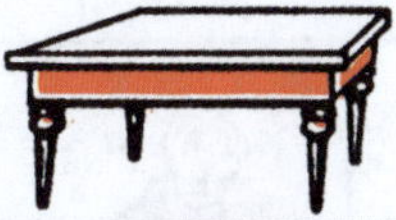	t
	n		u
	o		v
	p		w
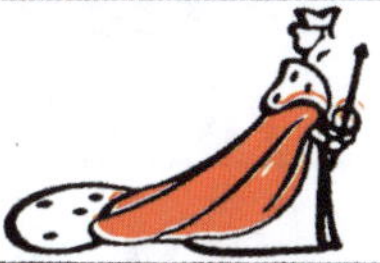	q	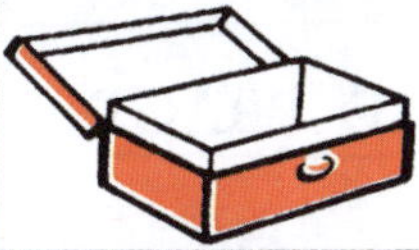	x
	r	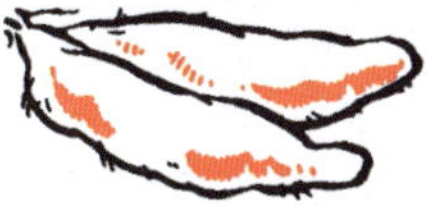	y
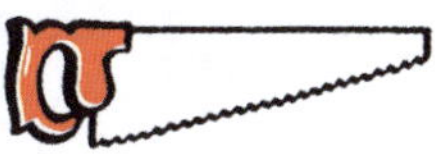	s		z

EASY TWO-LETTER WORDS

Note.—The pupil should pronounce the sound of each letter separately, and then combine them into one word, thus : i—n, i–n, in.

in	on	at	up
if	ox	am	us
it	of	an	
is		as	

FOR SOUND PRACTICE WITHOUT PICTURES

a	e	i	o	u
f	k	l	t	h
s	c	r	m	n
z	w	v	b	d
j	y	p	q	g

(Vowel sounds are all *short* vowels at present.)

FORMING THREE-LETTER WORDS

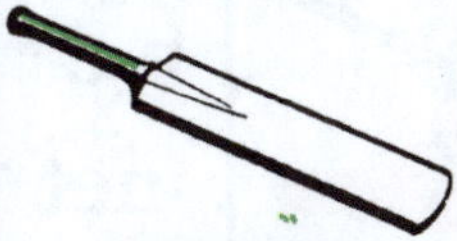	b-a-t bat		c-a-n can
	b-a-g bag		c-u-p cup
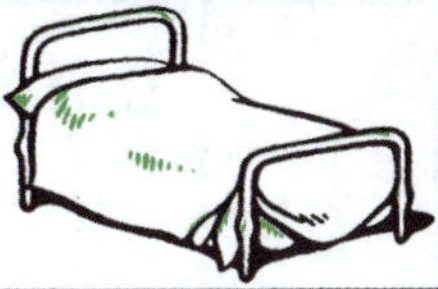	b-e-d bed		m-a-n man
	b-u-n bun		m-a-t mat
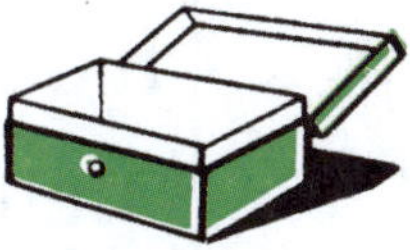	b-o-x box		m-u-g mug
	c-a-t cat		m-o-p mop
	c-a-p cap		f-a-n fan

FORMING THREE-LETTER WORDS

	p-a-n pan		n-e-t net
	p-e-n pen		j-a-m jam
	p-i-n pin		h-u-t hut
	p-i-g pig		v-a-n van
	d-o-g dog		h-e-n hen
	h-a-t hat		s-u-n sun
	r-a-t rat		l-e-g leg

EASY "LOOK AND SAY" WORDS

Note.—These short words introduce vowel sounds which have not been learned so far. The pupil should be trained to recognize them as *whole* words. In this book all "look and say" words are underlined. This will aid the child in recognizing them. (Teach I = i. " I " by itself says its own name.)

1. at the hut.
2. by the bed.
3. to the dog.
4. in the van.
5. on the box.

6. in the cup.
7. to the rat.
8. on the bed.
9. by the sun.
10. at the net.

over   under   with   from

1. with the cat.
2. over the hat.
3. from the bag.
4. under the cap.
5. over the mat.

6. by the fan.
7. in the mug.
8. with the man.
9. from the hen.
10. under the box.

CAPITAL LETTERS

Note.—These letters should be learned gradually when they are used in sentences. The pupil can refer to this page for any unknown capital, as it is placed by the small letter which is known.

Aa	Bb	Cc	Dd
Ee	Ff	Gg	Hh
Ii	Jj	Kk	Ll
Mm	Nn	Oo	Pp
Qq	Rr	Ss	Tt
Uu	Vv	Ww	Xx
	Yy	Zz	

He can run. Can he run to the cat. Yes.

He can sit. Can he sit on the tub. Yes.

She can hop. Can she hop to the box.

I can see the bed. A hat is on the bed.

She has a hat. Do you see the hat.

He can go by me. He has no cap.

He has a net for me.
I can see his net.

She has a bag.
I can not see it.
It is under the mat.

He put his hat on
the peg.
It was on his peg.

The dog is with the
cat.
The dog and the cat
are on the mat.

Do you see the dog.
Yes.   I do.

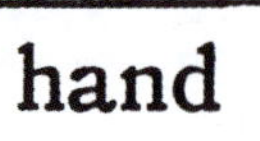

hand   sand   ant

Tim has an ant.

The ant is on his hand.

Tot has not an ant. It is in the sand.

Has Tim an ant on his hand. Yes, he has.

("Look and Say" words are underlined.)

got
hot
not
pot
lot

hot   pot   lot

Tim is hot.

Tot is not so hot.

Is Tot on the sand.   Yes.

Tot has sand in the pot.

Is the sand hot.   No.

It is not hot.

PICTURE AND SENTENCE MATCHING

Note.—The pupil should read the sentences and then say to which picture each sentence refers.

Dad is in the van.
Is Tom on the box.
His dog was under the van.

The jug has no lid.
Is the lid on the mat.
A rat was in the jug.

Has he a cap in his hand.
He has no cap on.
Is he big. Yes.

Has she a big fan.
Yes.   The fan is in
her hand.
The fan is for her.

We can see the box
and the tub.
The tub is by the
box.
Is the dog on the
box or the tub.

I see the sun.
It is up in the
sky.
The sun is over
the hut.

at
hat
sat
pat
fat
mat

cat

rat

sat

Tim sat on his hat.
Tim is not fat.
Is Tot fat. No.
Tot sat on the mat by the
    fat cat.
Can Tot pat the fat cat.
Yes, she can.

Note.—(1) "a" by itself says its own name.   (2) Easy words are not always **short**.   An occasional long word can be introduced by a picture.

dig
pig
fig
jig
big
wig

pig

fig

dance

Can a big pig dance.
Can a pig dance a jig.
A big pig can dance a jig in
  a wig for a fig.
Tim and Tot can dance for
  a fig. Have you a fig. No.

hut
nut

up
cup

pup
sup

Tim is up in the hut.
Tot let the pup sup.
The pup can sup from the
cup.
Tot and Tim can sup from
the cup in the hut.

am
jam
Sam
Pam
ham
yam

ham

jar

like

Sam and Pam like jam.
Tim and Tot like ham.
Is the ham in a jar.
No.   The jam is in a jar.
I like ham and jam.
Has Pam a yam.   No.

19

The rat is in the
pan.
It is not on the
rug.
The rat got under
the rug.

Do you see a yam.
Put the yam in
the pot.
It is hot in the
pot.

Sam has a bad
leg.
He put a pin in
his leg.
Go to bed, Sam.

The egg is by the
hen.
She is a big hen.
Can she run. Yes.

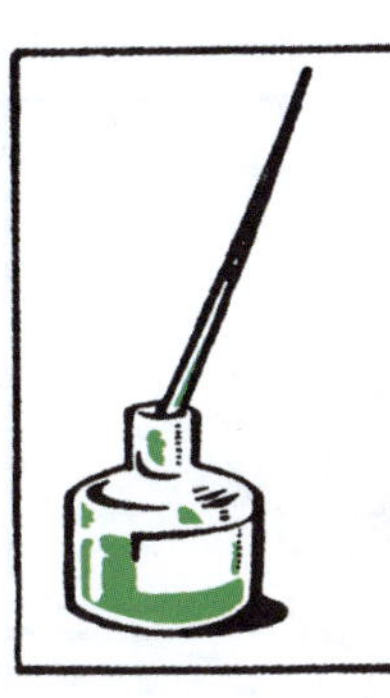

I see the ink.
The pen is in the
ink.
Is it red ink. No.

Tom has a bat.
It is in his hand.
He can hit the ball,
so! We have it.

net
pet
met
let
set
get

lamb

wet   yet

Tot met a lamb.
Did Tot get a lamb as a
    pet. Yes, she did.
Tim did not get a pet.
Let Tim get a can.
Tim set a can on a mat.

dog
log
hog

fig
dig
big

lost

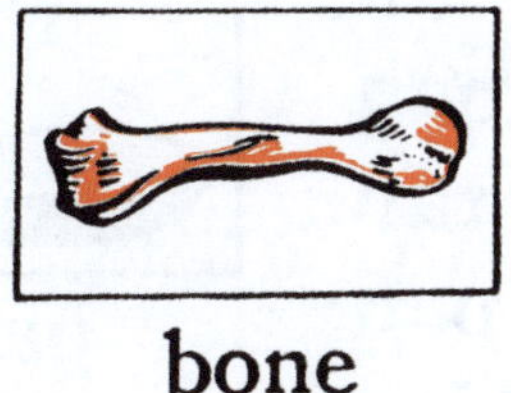

bone

("e" has no sound).

Tim has a dog. He let the
dog sit on a log.
Tot has lost her pet dog.
The big dog lost a bone.
Tim let the dog dig for it.

an
man
ran
pan
Dan
van

pan

drive

Dan is the man in the van.

A pan is in the van.

Tot got a pan from Dan.

Tim ran to Dan in the van.

Dan let Tim drive the van.

ox

box

top

The ox is big.
Tim is not so big. Tim is
on a box by the ox.
A dog is by the box.
Can the ox hop to the top
of the box.

I am thin and sad. Can I run on the road. No. I had a tin of thin milk but no meat. I am fond of meat.

I am fat and glad. I am a pug dog. I have meat and milk and bread, but no fish. Pug dogs do not eat fish.

I run.   I sit.
He runs. He sits.
She runs.
She sits.

Did he run to the hut.   Yes.
Tim sits by the box.
We stand in the hot sun.
He jumps over a rat.
You run to her.   She sits
with her pet cat.

I stand.
I jump.
He stands.
He jumps.
She stands.
She jumps.

27

Ben
hen
men
den
pen
ten

den

ten

A hen is in the pen.
A dog runs to the pen.
The dog runs to his den
with a hen.
Tim runs to the men.
Ten men run to the den of
the dog. We are glad.

un
b**un**
f**un**
s**un**
r**un**

bun

sun

stand

It is fun to run in the sun.
Tim can stand in the sun.
Run, Tim, run.
Tot has a bun.
She can run to Tim with the
bun.

Note.—The second "l" has no sound.

bell		ill	
tell		bill	
fell		fill	
well	bell	hill	mill
sell		mill	
doll	kill	pill	will

Tot is ill. She had a pill.
Will you tell him to sell the
doll. We will have it.
He fell in the well.
The mill is by a hill.
Tim has a bill.
Tot runs to the bell.
Fill the box
with sand.

WORD LIST (FOR REVISION)

Phonetic.			*" Look and Say."*	
at	and	cup	are	go
hat	hand	pup	you	so
it	ant	get	for	she
pit	ox	met	was	the
am	box	yet	put	by
yam	rug	fun	over	my
hen	jug	sun	under	jar
men	fat	gun	from	egg
ten	rat	tin	with	sky
Dad	pig	thin	bone	lost
had	fig	bag	ball	lamb
lad	nut	mug	like	her
dog	hut	fan	jump	were
log	bed	ran	stand	eat
not	red	yes	shoot	meat
got	top	see	dance	have
leg	hop	runs	to	drive
beg	mop	sits	do	milk
fell	kill	doll	fond	fish
well	will	tell	glad	road

OXFORD
UNIVERSITY PRESS

Great Clarendon Street, Oxford, OX2 6DP, United Kingdom

Oxford University Press is a department of the University of Oxford.
It furthers the University's objective of excellence in research, scholarship,
and education by publishing worldwide. Oxford is a registered trade mark of
Oxford University Press in the UK and in certain other countries

The moral rights of the authors have been asserted

First published by Nelson Thornes Ltd
This edition published by Oxford University Press in 2014

British Library Cataloguing in Publication Data
Data available

978-0-1756-6001-8

45

Printed in China by Shanghai Offset Printing Products Ltd